Agent
to
Agent

"Professional" Cooperation

Agent to Agent

"Professional" Cooperation

by

Pat Ford, Bachelor of Science

Vice-President, Broker, CPPS, CMRS, CRS, CSP, GRI

DORRANCE
PUBLISHING CO
EST. 1920
PITTSBURGH, PENNSYLVANIA 15238

Dorrance Publishing Co
585 Alpha Drive
Pittsburgh, PA 15238
Visit our website at www.dorrancebookstore.com

ISBN: 978-1-6386-7341-5
eISBN: 978-1-6386-7368-2

BACKGROUND

Pat is a **native Memphian** who moved to the Nashville area, in 1995 as a result of a relocation initiative involving her family. She currently resides in Columbia, TN is a member of Mt. Calvary MB Church, where she is Vice-President of the **Board of Trustees**, and **Ministry Leader** of the Women's Missionary Ministry.

EDUCATION:

Attended Shelby **State Community College Memphis, Tennessee Under-graduate Junior Memphis State University**

Transferred to **Middle Tennessee State University (MTSU), now a graduate with a "Bachelor of Science" degree in Liberal Studies.**

Started her real estate career in **1984,**

To date: She has 37 years of experience

ACHIEVEMENTS IN REAL ESTATE:

Broker's License in 1987

Vice-President Crye-Leike Realtors 1999

Graduate of the Realtor's Institute **(GRI)**

Graduate of the Dale Carnegie Institute Sales Program

Certified Residential Specialist **(CRS)**

Certified New Homes Sales Professional **(CSP)**

Certified Military Residential Specialist **(CMRS)**

Certified Premier Property Specialist **(CPPS)**

Four year Awards of Excellence recipient **GNAR**

Life member of the Crye-Leike Multi-Dollar Club

Circle of Excellence recipient Crye-Leike Realtors

TEACHING EXPERIENCE CONTINUED:

Certified Instructor Tennessee Association of Realtors **(TAR)**

Past Instructor: **Nashville School of Real Estate**

Past Instructor: **Orientation** at the Greater Nashville Association of Realtors **(GNAR)** as a member.

Past Volunteer Tutor: The **Adult Literacy Council**, Nashville, Tennessee

Past **Volunteer Teacher of new agents** at our **Franklin office** with contract classes, and **recent** Volunteer Teacher of contract classes in our **Spring Hill office for new agents**. Shared **"Thriving in Today's Market"** a revised presentation **reproduced and reprinted** by her to give the Spring Hill office agents tips from a seminar attended in Chattanooga, TN presented by **Rick Deluca.**

Hobbies: Bowling, Golf

Developed her own course: **"Agent to Agent Cooperation."**
A copyright for this course is approved.

TABLE OF CONTENTS

Preface

The idea for writing this book came to pass while experiencing so many serious situations during transactions with real estate agents around the years starting 2009-2010. Those situations shed so much light on interactions with agents that seemed to be clueless about what and how to perform their side of the transaction. In some cases it was deemed necessary to perform both sides of the transaction to get them to come to fruition.

Other ideas for this book developed from a course that is copyrighted, "Agent to Agent Cooperation," also recognized by the TREC and myself certified as the Instructor. The ideas in the course are those needed to be brought into the open for all Realtors/real estate agents to recognize their importance. In addition, the need to take into consideration that it is our successful efforts of "cooperation" with each other that make a "dream" come true for our clients and customers. It takes teamwork to bring it all together to make a closing successful and result in a happy ending. Andrew Carnegie once said, "Teamwork is the ability to work together toward a common vision. The ability to direct individual accomplishments toward organizational objectives. It is the fuel that allows common people to attain uncommon results."

It is important to note that all of us have different personalities, ideologies, cultures, and the like. Moreover, it is how we embrace the understanding that we are all "different," and because we are, it should not impede the ability to understand each other or undermine our efforts to do our very best to be professional from start to finish of a transaction.

In conclusion, showing our "professionalism" and the way we intend to conduct ourselves while working towards a "hassle free" closing should be the goal. To reach that goal it takes preparation, knowledge, patience, understanding, temperance, kindness, self-control, and steadfastness. When we can demonstrate these qualities during the course of the cooperation efforts, then we can say, everything was done on my part to the best of my ability. ⟨

Signed
Pat Ford
Bachelor of Science (B.S.)
Vice-President, Broker, CMRS, CPPS, CRS, CSP, GRI
Crye-Leike Inc. Realtors

Acknowledgements

I would like to acknowledge all of the clients and customers with whom I have had the honor of serving during my career. I also want to thank the Realtors with whom I have cooperated in a host of transactions. Those transactions have helped me become better at recognizing the need for understanding and patience when it comes to working through issues and cooperating with other agents.

Appreciation is also given to the many loan officers, appraisers, and home inspectors that have shown their professionalism when we needed them to step up and be a "beacon of light" when issues would inevitably show up to make a good transaction look like it was developing into a "nightmare."

My hat is also off to the closing agents who made the finalization of the transaction go smoothly for the clients and customers.

Without the help of all of the aforementioned, my experiences in real estate may not have prompted me to write this book for all to recognize just how fragile it can become, when we fail to do our very best to make "cooperation" a top priority.

With heartfelt gratitude, I want to express my sincere thanks to Jeremiah Baker, the Professional Graphic Designer who works at Crye-Leike Realtors. His diligent efforts and design work have made the front and the back cover of my book outstanding.

William Arthur Ward, an inspirational writer once said, "Feeling gratitude and not expressing it is like wrapping a present and not giving it."

"The LAW of Authenticity"

"As long as you're trying to be someone else, or putting on some act or behavior someone else taught you, you have no possibility of truly reaching people" (The "Go-Giver", Bob Burg and John David Mann, 2007, 2015).

While we are working each and every transaction to the best of our ability, are we taking time to actually "reach" other people? Or, are we in it for just ourselves? This is a question we can ask ourselves and then decide which outcome fits the behavior we have come to know about ourselves and our fellow agents. Each agent has their own duties to perform. Understanding what to do and when is crucial for the cooperation efforts to be sustainable.

"The most valuable thing you have to give people is yourself." "No matter what you think you are selling, what you are really offering is you" (The "Go-Giver," Bob Burg and John David Mann, 2007, 2015).

What do we value the most when it comes down to how we want to be remembered? Do we want to be thought of as one who put the customer or client first? Or, do we want to be remembered as thinking only of ourselves when it came down to what really mattered the most?

C.S. Lewis a British writer once said, "True humility is not thinking less of yourself, it's thinking of yourself less." ✕

This Book is...

Intended to increase your **thought patterns** about "**HOW**" you do business.

- It is intended to help you treat your **"fellow Realtor"** with **respect,** and about giving them a good **feeling** about the sale of your listings.
- In addition, it is intended to help you **grow your business** as a result thereof, causing you to have **"repeat"** Buyers and Sellers.
- Also, it is intended to **create harmony** among agents and give them the desire to show other agent's **listings and cooperate** with them in the hopes of coming to a **successful** closed transaction.

This Book is NOT...

Intended to take the place of the necessary **teaching needed from your Principal Broker** when you are unsure of what to do.

Nor is it intended to have you **ignore what your duties** are to a client or customer as they are written in your Buyer's agency agreement and or listing agreement.

Chapter One

Welcome to *Agent to Agent "Professional" Cooperation*. This book is designed to enhance your thought patterns that relate to **"HOW"** you do business. In addition, it is intended to help you treat your **"fellow Realtor"** with respect giving them a good feeling about the sale of your listings. It is also intended to help you **grow your business** as a result thereof, causing you to have more Buyers and Sellers.

Moreover, the intent is to help create harmony among agents. In addition, give them the desire to show their fellow agent's listings and cooperate with them to the best of their ability. With this in mind, there will be the potential of having a successfully closed transaction.

First, let's examine the three scenarios starting with our "thought patterns." When we think in a particular way, our thought patterns are at work. Enhancing these thoughts in such a way that they accentuate the positive and minimize the negative can possibly keep a transaction from "going south." No matter how much you might like to ask the agent, "What part of this do you not understand?" The most important part of our actions during the negotiations is our patience and understanding of how "different" we are and how we do not "negotiate" the same. Remaining as positive as we can about the outcome can cause it to come to fruition. No matter how many times the "counter-offer" comes back worded a "different way" but asking for the "same thing," continue to work together to make it a success.

Consider **"critical thinking"** and make it the forefront of those thoughts. When this is done effectively, then we can view them as a collection of many factors. Those would include analysis, interpretation, open-mindedness, and problem-solving. Moreover, when we have an opportunity to serve the needs of Buyers and Sellers, a crucial element to make that service successful is "cooperation." Thus, while we are going back and forth in the negotiations, remember to treat each other with respect. Embracing this element of critical thinking can catalyze, meaning looking for the good points of the offer, and not concentrating solely on the parts that are not agreeable. Also, we need to interpret upfront the actual intent of the terms before trying to present them to either Buyer or Seller. Then, keeping an open mind to what, if anything needs to be addressed to make it acceptable. Last, solving the inevitable problems takes "cooperation."

Cooperation, by definition, is "the actions of someone who is being helpful by doing what is wanted or asked for" Merriam Webster, Inc. 2018. When we decide to cooperate to the best of our ability, we take ourselves out of the negotiation and leave the Buyers and Sellers to make decisions with guidance from us on the "best foot forward." Those actions that we perform when we are helpful and doing what our Buyer or Seller wants are in the realm of cooperating. We should do so to the very best of our ability, then leave our "attitudes" about what is being negotiated out of the conversation. What could happen if we don't, might be to the detriment of our client or customer and would not serve them well.

Harmony and good feelings about the other agent create the desire to show the listings of the other agent due to what has transpired in the past. The desire is to maintain that harmony to have future sales with all agents and great expectations to work together "again" soon! Sending constant updates to the agent while the transaction is in progress and staying abreast of every facet of the transaction shows professionalism at its highest point. Then topping it off with a thank you card when the sale is complete puts the "icing on the cake" and may keep you "Top of Mind," remembering how you work and how well you communicate.

Moreover, when the Buyer and/or Seller observes how you conduct yourself in a negotiation, they have an opportunity to evaluate your "character" at work, and they can see how you work things out when their situation becomes dire. Remember the **"Golden Rule**?" "Do unto others as you would have them do unto you." What would you want to happen if you were the Buyer or Seller? How would you want to be treated? Would you want to be treated professionally? A good ending for negotiations would mean the Buyer and Seller won. If this premise holds true, then they will feel better about sending you referrals. Moreover, the other agent will be happy to show your listings when the opportunity presents itself.

Here is a quote to peruse. "That word is 'willing.' It's an attitude and spirit of cooperation that should permeate our conversations. It's like a palm tree by the ocean that endures the greatest winds because it knows how to gracefully bend," Stephen Kendrick, *The Love Dare*. Pondering this and thinking about this word "willing" makes cooperation more and more significant to the success of transactions and the very process in which they are brought to fruition. "Gracefully bend" does not necessarily mean giving in, but taking the time to think about what the other side is trying to convey when making an effort to communicate. Both sides in a negotiation will need to "bend" or give a little to make the offer work. ☙

Chapter Two

You have found the home for them!

What do you do first?

Do you immediately get your offer in to the listing agent, via email, and wait for them to respond to you? Or, do you call or text the agent, to make sure they are aware you sent an offer via email? Both questions are important. The important part is what you do upfront by verifying the "status" of the property with the listing agent *before* you write the offer. Also, preparing a (CMA) Comparable Market Analysis is part of your due diligence for the Buyer to assist in making a viable offer.

Working with the Buyer and Seller is where your **cooperation** efforts manifest themselves and show how well you can work with the other agent. When you notice the agent involved is one you cooperated with in the past, what do you do? Remember the good experience last time, and say I know this will go over well because "I know how they work."

Or, does this happen, you say *oh no*, this is the home they desire, but I know what happened the last time I tried to work with that agent. It was a terrible nightmare! We can transform our image from one that is "frowned upon" by fellow agents to one that is "accepted." We can start with having a "change of heart." When you change the way you feel about something, your actions will reflect in that change. Actions that change because your heart caused it should mean that you may see things from a different perspective and want to have a better outcome in your negotiations. Having a mentality of "**one and done**" could mean thoughts about a transaction might possibly be construed as, "this may be the only one that I will be working on with this agent." It doesn't matter what the outcome will be. This type of mentality could not be further from the truth. Inevitably, your paths will cross again. Do not regret the opportunity to present an offer to the agent or accept one from them. Embrace the opportunity to work together again, and strive for a better outcome.

A choice is made every day about how we will conduct ourselves at work and around others. Our day could start with "giving thanks to God" for allowing another day in our lives. Then start the day with a thankful heart and observe how habits can take on a "new image" from the outset of the "cooperation."

First, let's take a look at how building a "new image" can foster great cooperation experiences. A good cooperative spirit can maximize our efforts when we are aware of how our behavior, words, and disposition play a significant role. While you are negotiating, a contract can change due to inspection findings or the appraisal. The period of "Resolution" is at hand, comments such as, your Seller being "hard pressed to find someone to pay cash," a Buyer will not "waive the right to an appraisal or something is only worth what someone is willing to pay" have no place in conversation. These statements during a resolution of terms of a contract should make the person stop for a moment and think *before* responding. Or, deliberately *not* respond at all to those types of comments. Should these comments be given a response, then the negotiation is no longer between the Buyer and Seller. It is now a back and forth between the agents with their attitudes about the "would-be Buyer," which has no place in the conversation, since we already have a Buyer.

Moreover, one way to have a "feel good" moment for the agent would be to send them a "thank you note" for the offer, in the beginning. That will set the tone for the beginning of cooperation and let them know you are going to do your best to get their offer to work. Let the Buyer's agent know "how" you work as you keep them informed via email or text message with updates. Also that their offer will receive as much priority as all offers you may have or will have pending. Stay in touch with the other agent as much as possible to assure them you are on top of the transaction and doing everything possible to make it work. When the listing agent says, "We are going to do this!" It means for everyone we are a team. "Teamwork begins by building trust. And the only way to do that is to overcome our need for invulnerability," Patrick Lencioni. One thing to note about this comment is the word "invulnerability." We will be attacked in one form or another, in this life. We are "vulnerable" whether we like it or not. It is our character and perseverance within that gives us the strength to sustain the attacks, the failures, and downfalls that make us who we are and gives us the ability to strive for success in every transaction and to make the next one better than the last.

I heard a loan officer say, "Teamwork makes the dream work." Being all about making the "dream work" takes a team effort. Cooperation has been successful when both agents find themselves searching for solutions to make the transaction work. Take a look at this scenario. The Buyer has been denied a loan. The "Seller's" agent offers help with using a lender they know well and believe they can get the loan approved. They recommended the lender, and the Buyer's loan progress looks better with the new lender. The Seller agrees to an extension to close due to the hard work and dedication of the new lender referred by their agent.

What we see in this scenario is a Buyer declined, and the help of the Seller's agent. The Buyer's agent stayed in touch with regular updates about the Buyer's attempts to get approved, but was turned down after several weeks, and the loan progress had gone so far that an appraisal had been done. With all of what has just transpired with the Buyer, "well wishes" of the Seller's agent begin to transform the situation with words like, "Let me see how I can help." Cooperation is at its highest when *both* agents feel the need to work together for the common goal. That common goal is making the dream come true for the client and customer. "Alone we can do little; together we can do so much," Helen Keller.

In conclusion, keep in mind what everyone wants, a "Win-Win-Win" situation. Then focus on doing our part to make it happen, striving each day not only to make a living, but make the dreams come true for all of those who place their faith and trust in us as Realtors and Real estate agents.

Chapter Three

What should we, as agents, look for in the Offer while negotiating?

Let's take a moment to review how this element of a transaction affects cooperation and some "Rules of Thumb" that will keep you at peak performance. First, review the terms and conditions of the offer presented yourself *before* you present it to your Seller. Why would you do this you might say? There is an old saying, " An ounce of prevention is worth a pound of cure." When the agents work together to iron out the intent of what is written in the offer beforehand, it can save a lot of time and effort on both sides.

Ways to perform a review involve highlighting all pertinent aspects of the offer, especially those where you have blanks to fill in and where blanks have *not* been filled. For example, if the Buyer asks for closing costs and enters an amount, and also wants title expense paid, does that amount *include* the title expense? If so, it would be a good idea to say, "This amount includes the cost for title insurance." In the case of an **FHA** or **VA** loan, does the lender charge fees the Buyer cannot pay, the Seller will have to pay? The Buyer's agent should know this. If they are not sure, ask them to find out and make it clear so that there is no ambiguity about what is being agreed upon. Be sure to make all offers clear and concise, even if it means adding a "counteroffer" to avoid misunderstandings about the Seller costs and Buyer costs.

Moreover, what are some "**Good Rules of Thumb**" to remember? As mentioned earlier at the beginning of this chapter, the need to review the offer *before* it is presented, and a good rule of thumb started here. Can you imagine what it would be like if you discovered the content of the offer the same time as the Seller and did not make yourself aware of what you are presenting to the Seller? Doing due diligence to get unanswered questions beforehand makes your presentation much more professional. Always take the time to ask about blanks in the offer left unanswered or information that is ambiguous. How does this important element during the progression of the transaction affect cooperation? Let's examine closely some "Good Rules of Thumb" to answer this important question. There are two to look at closely.

Good Rule of Thumb #1
In the spirit of **cooperation** an effort is made to show the other agent that you are a professional. Also that you want the offer to be given the best effort. The Listing agent should do the following, in addition to what they know is required by our Code. They should acknowledge receipt of the offer, and thank the agent for the offer. Then, after contacting the Seller and determining a date and time it will be presented, notify the Buyer's agent of same.

At the time of acknowledgement of the offer, there are some crucial details that should not be overlooked and are listed below:

(1.) **A review of the offer**, as mentioned in the **due diligence** above, should be done and any provisions written in the offer clarified so that when it is presented to the Seller you already know the answer. That makes the negotiating less complicated and less time spent on reviewing.

If you represent the Seller, take a blank piece of paper and write the offer terms out one by one to know them specifically. Leave nothing out of the negotiating. Start with the property address, Tax ID information for verification, special stipulations, and all the way to the "Time limit" of the offer. Having reviewed this information before you sit down with the Seller shows your professionalism and gives confidence to the Seller that you have their best interest at heart when it comes to negotiating their expected expenses.

In the case of a Buyer's representative, make sure you have read the offer thoroughly and you know the offer terms and conditions that you have had your Buyer submit for acceptance. How would it sound to the Buyer if you had to say to the listing agent, "I didn't know we had that checked?" This is referring to any particular part of the offer you have had the Buyer sign. Or, if you fail to mention to the Seller that the Buyer is asking for **title costs** and **closing costs** to be paid, and they failed to read it for themselves.

More often than not, the Buyer nor the Seller is aware of what they are signing, and are counting on the agent to guide them through the details and the fine print of the many pages of legal wording, they have probably never read or heard before. Is this a *red flag*? We can agree it is!

Good Rule of Thumb #2

(2.) Send the Buyer's agent a thank you text or email acknowledging your appreciation for the offer. Either of these expressions of appreciation work and make the agent feel special that you took the time to do it. Take time to explain in your answer if it is the case you have an assistant, and he or she may be doing follow-ups on your behalf regarding the details of the transaction, and what has transpired thus far. Or, that you work with a "co-list" agent and the file will be theirs to maintain, and they can expect to receive calls from the co-list agent as well as the listing agent, if necessary.

Note: It is alright to have the assistant call with "updates" from time to time, but ultimately, it is the Seller's agent and Buyer's agent responsibility to *know* what is going on with the file at *all* times! That includes both listing and co-listing agent.

During the negotiations, make sure to respond in a timely fashion especially within the timeframe stated in the contract. If for some reason the Seller or Buyer cannot respond within the timeframe in the offer, do not ignore it and hope it is not noticed or it is not necessary to abide by it. Advise the other agent of the same. It will be necessary to extend your time limit to keep your contract enforceable. If the time limit runs out, the contract reads, "Offer terminates if not countered or accepted by" whatever time is entered in that blank space of the contract.

Listing Agent and Buyer's agents remember:

1. The contract/offer is between the **Buyer** and **Seller**, and *not* the agents!
2. It is not about *us*.
3. We are not to do the "blame game" or point out what each other "did" or "did not" do.
4. Never enter information for acceptance without placing it on a counteroffer form, or addendum if it needs to be an addition to the agreement. Any addition or revision, becomes a counter-offer or amendment and it cannot be treated as "information only," by adding it to the contract in hopes it won't be seen as a change.
5. If the offer does not work out, we should take time to thank the other agent for their cooperation, and wish them the best towards their future transactions.
6. Being professional is what makes Buyers and Sellers respect and want to keep us when they are ready to buy again, or sell again. It also makes the agent with which you just cooperated respect you for your Professionalism.

Another cooperation effort involves the handling of a "Multiple Offer Situation."

What about the handling of these types of offers? You are to be guided by the rules for those types that are provided by the seller. In the spirit of cooperation, the Listing agent acknowledges after a second offer is received that there is a "multiple offer situation" that is now in place for accepting offers. The multiple offer form allows the agent to give a time and date provided by the Seller for each Buyer to give their highest and best offer.

In conclusion, what can be said about the transactions? Bob Burg and John David Mann put it this way: "Our approach is aimed at making the sale, while our goal is always to create value," (*Go-Givers Sell More*, p. 155). Buyers and Sellers want to feel their best interest is being taken into consideration since this is most likely the largest investment they may ever make. ⟆

Chapter Four

The Binding Agreement

From this point we will review what has now occurred with the offer. It has worked out and has become a Binding Agreement. Here is where the breadth and depth of the cooperation efforts start. Timelines are crucial, as they are mentioned over and over again and cannot be stressed enough.

The agent with the final counter offer enters the Binding Agreement date. If the offer is accepted with no counteroffer, it is signed by the Seller, and the listing agent sends it back to the Buyer's agent upon acceptance and the Buyer's agent enters the Binding Agreement date and time. As long as we have the Binding Agreement date and time, we know there is a fully executed contract. The agent who has entered this date and time should contact the other agent to advise of the date and time entered and send back that page.

We have forms already prepared that show us the crucial negotiated dates and times. These are to be in compliance with the terms of the contract. We can prepare our own for reference. Should a decision be made to prepare your own, then careful scrutiny should be done to make sure nothing is left out.

Over the years, the Buyer's and Seller's itinerary have helped and served well to help the Buyer and Seller stay abreast of what is happening during the transaction. These are important from the home inspection to the final inspection. Some examples of what is included in a Buyer's itinerary would be when the earnest money is due, their loan commitment letter due date, if not already provided, their home owner's insurance, the estimated appraisal date, closing date, and more.

What does this document do for the Buyer during the transaction you might ask? It saves a lot of time and effort, since they now have a "checklist" of their own to stay on track, and make them feel in control of the duties needed to make the sale successful. There may be some that will "shy away from it," but allow them an opportunity to make their own judgment whether they want it or not.

Now we take a look at the Buyer's Agent duties to perform. In the spirit of cooperation, these duties should be done to the best of their ability, without compromise. Let's look at these three preliminary items:

1. Take note in the contract about delivering the earnest money to the listing agent. The listing agent is so appreciative of this part. The Buyer's agent took the time to say that it is being delivered on a particular date and time. This exudes professionalism by the Buyer's agent.
2. Second, take note of the days agreed when the lender pre-approval letter is due, and the days for the Buyer's loan application. Remember, the listing agent has to update the Seller on what is happening here with the Buyer's ability to purchase the home. There should not be any ambiguity about the Buyer's qualification that has not been communicated between the two agents.

3. When the Buyer's agent updates the listing agent within the first one or two days that, the earnest money will be provided on a particular date, and the home inspection is being done by a date decided, it is exemplary evidence and a good indication that the agent has "all their ducks in a row" and expects to be very cooperative and cognizant of timelines and contract conformity.

Working together and cooperating within the constraints of the offer makes the transaction go smoothly and keeps everyone in synchronization with what is happening and keeps the atmosphere flowing smoothly. We hope to get "smiley face" responses in the text messages and "thumbs-up" as a way of showing appreciation of the work done. We strive to keep a good atmosphere while getting the job done.

Moreover, how the Buyer and Seller feel about the progress with the transaction should be a concern of both the Listing agent and Buyer's agent. Let's take a look at the Buyer first. Have you ever heard a Buyer say, "The agent never called me to say what was going on with the transaction. I had to call the Seller's agent to find out what was going on!" Also, how disheartening would it be to hear, "They never told me it was not going to close until the day of closing!" Here is the question. How is this "performing duties" of either agent when there is a customer that does not understand what is going on?

Now let's look at the Listing agent's duties. Here are three preliminary items to consider.

1. Make sure the timelines in the contract are written on a checklist to keep you intact. Prepare a list of what is due and when it is to be done.
2. Anticipate the actions of the Buyer's agent to verify they are aware of the duties to cooperate that you have part of your checklist.
3. Make sure the earnest/trust money is provided. Verify that it is within the timeframe of the contract. Contact the Seller to advise them of receipt and deposit of the funds.

Again, working together to get these preliminary duties off to a good start sets the stage for well wishes. Look towards the "next sale" with this agent while concentrating on how well the agent responds to their present duties.

As mentioned earlier there are certain forms that can help keep your customers and clients in the loop. What is the "Seller's Itinerary?"

The Seller's Itinerary spells out specifically what will transpire from the date of the executed contract to closing. It will explain to the Seller what they need to do to fulfill their contractual duties. An example would be to make sure the utilities are on if there is an inspection to be done. If it is a VA loan, the Seller is now responsible to provide a termite letter for the Buyer. This Itinerary gives the Seller a checklist of their own to keep up with the details, and makes them feel they are in control of their side of the transaction.

What is the "Buyer's Itinerary?" Like the Seller's Itinerary, it gives the Buyer control of the tasks necessary to help the agents cooperate with each other by doing their part. For example:

1. Making sure the pre-approval letter is provided to the agent.
2. Providing the earnest/trust money within the time limit.
3. Deciding on the home inspector to use for purposes of a home inspection during the timeframe agreed upon in the contract and more.

The importance of using these documents can't be stressed enough when you have at your fingertips the difference between having a "smooth" transaction and having one with "bumps in the road."

Cooperation efforts stay strong and intact when there is a plan of action. The duties of each agent are agreed upon coupled with a desire to get to a successful transaction.

The next and final chapter will summarize what we can do together to make all of our hard work come to fruition.

Chapter Five

What do we do as Real Estate Professionals?

Let's think about the principles we have just learned from the four chapters in this book. When an agent presents an offer on our listing, or when we present our next offer to one of our fellow agents; let's remember how we can professionally go through the process from start to finish.

First, we start, or "begin with the end in mind," as Stephen Covey so eloquently states in his book, the *7 Habits of Highly Effective People*. We want a strong start with the presentation, robust performance with lots of "smiley faces" and "thumbs-up" so we can get to a very effective ending that will reap additional opportunities with this agent and all of the other agents they know and will tell about their experience.

We discussed three scenarios involving thought patterns, how different we are, and the fact that we do not negotiate the same. Moreover, we contextualized the "critical thinking" aspect that could bring out the "good points" of an offer to look at *first* to set the stage for an effective outcome.

Second, we want *all* parties to have a "happy ending," so they will tell all their family, friends, and loved ones about it and have them wish for the same experience. There is a saying, "The measure of a man is not how he lives with success, but how he lives with failures." Our goal is to constantly strive to measure the "successes" and minimize whenever possible the failures. But, should we fail, we will rise up, dust ourselves off, and try again. This led us to the word "willing" that inspired the belief that an attitude and spirit of cooperation should permeate our conversations as we strive to make our transactions come to fruition.

Third, the process of cooperation at the start can take on a good and comfortable beginning when we do not allow past interaction with an agent to interfere with the present effort to serve our Client or Customer. Though efforts to work with and cooperate with a particular agent did not work out as well as we thought, it should not be a reason to refuse to work with them again.

Then, we reviewed "Rules of Thumb" to go by when an offer is submitted to the Listing agent and the actions that should be taken to bring about successful "cooperation." These rules served to make efforts as Professional as possible while we make every effort to let each other know how we work and what we plan to do to keep each other informed about the transaction as we move forward.

Finally, the fourth chapter teaches what information we have at our disposal to provide for our Clients and Customers to keep abreast of the transaction, and give them opportunities to make sure they are in compliance with the terms of the contract. In addition, we spelled out "duties" of each agent as they performed what is expected on each side of the transaction.

Henry Ford once said, "**Coming** together is a beginning, **keeping** together is progress, **working** together is success." To put this in the context of a transaction, when the offer is presented, that is the "coming together," then the elements of the transaction that involve the due diligence of what the terms of the contract entail is the "keeping together." The contract can fall apart due to many factors. Then the "working together" is where both agents have found a "common ground" upon which to make the transaction a success because they learned to "cooperate" so well together.

I am very mindful of the fact that this book is being written during the Coronavirus pandemic. Many are losing their lives to this virus. Others make an effort each day to live their lives to the fullest and want the American dream of home ownership. I am aware too that it is incumbent upon us to cooperate more now than ever before. And, in the spirit of cooperation, we should keep our eyes on the "prize." What is the prize? It is the best outcome for all parties, a successful closing, a good feeling then and afterwards. The intent of our interactions should not be "one and done," but a top of mind progressive effort to maintain good thoughts and feelings that the "next sale is coming soon." That intent should also be a catalyst for more sales due to referrals. The clients and customers we serve have placed their faith and trust in us with a full appreciation of a job well done.

In conclusion, it has been with great honor that I have poured out my heartfelt beliefs and desires to address my thoughts about "cooperation." When efforts made between the two agents involved can come together no matter how much there is a difference of opinion on contract language, contract pricing, or even contract costs for either side, the final result should be the "understanding" on both sides that made the transaction work, and caused a happy ending. ✧